SEALED WITH LOVE : VOLUME 2

AF445788

NRITYANGANA KALA KENDRA

Copyright © Nrityangana Kala Kendra
All Rights Reserved.

ISBN 979-8886069877-7

This book has been published with all efforts taken to make the material error-free after the consent of the author. However, the author and the publisher do not assume and hereby disclaim any liability to any party for any loss, damage, or disruption caused by errors or omissions, whether such errors or omissions result from negligence, accident, or any other cause.

While every effort has been made to avoid any mistake or omission, this publication is being sold on the condition and understanding that neither the author nor the publishers or printers would be liable in any manner to any person by reason of any mistake or omission in this publication or for any action taken or omitted to be taken or advice rendered or accepted on the basis of this work. For any defect in printing or binding the publishers will be liable only to replace the defective copy by another copy of this work then available.

Enticing as it may sound,

Forever is a really long time.

Contents

Contents

Preface

Sealed With Love: Volume 2 is a collection of poetry that romanticizes the idea of love but at the same time puts it under the scrutiny of harsh reality.

The following collection contains poetry by Swarnika, Khushi Kaushik, and Raman Singh. This project has been taken up by and done under Nrityangana Kala Kendra. The editing and compilation of this book have been done by Swarnika.

Acknowledgements

The collection of poetry has beautifully shaped up with the contributions of the three poets of Sealed With Love: Volume 2.

I'd like to thank Khushi Kaushik and Raman Singh for their dedication and hard work as they took up this endeavor during the course of their internship with Nrityangana Kala Kendra. This collection lines up perfectly with its predecessor, Sealed With Love: Volume 1.

I'd also like to thank the reader who invests themselves with us as they read this collection. I sincerely hope that you would find yourself associating and resonating with the collection or at least a part of it.

Prologue

- Swarnika

I've sealed my love for you
Between the pages of this book.
I've masked my conscience
To probably get it off the hook.
I've let go of the idea of us
The deviance had me shook.
I've sealed and hidden this book today
Somewhere you won't ever look.

Swarnika

Swarnika is an avid reader and an ambivert. She is a glass-half-full kind of a person, not because she is always an optimist but because she believes that a glass that is full has no more scope and ends up creating the most amount of spills.

She completed her Bachelor's and Master's degree from the University of Delhi. She has completed her three-level professional certification in Spanish from Valencia Polytechnic University, Spain. She has also completed her certificate program in French from St. Stephen's College, University of Delhi. She is currently pursuing a Post-Graduate Diploma in Business Administration from Symbiosis Centre for Distance Learning, Pune. She is working on her thesis and research papers to earn her Ph.D. degree in English Literature. She has a keen interest in criminology and detective fiction. Writings that indulge mystery and rationale speak volumes to her. She has earned her TEFL and TESOL certificates as an English language teacher. She is also a certified dance teacher with specializations in Bharatnatyam, Kathak, and Contemporary. She is also certified in Classical Music and Fine Arts.

She believes in living in the moment rather than giving the moment the opportunity to live through you without you even realizing it. She has started her company- Nrityangana Kala Kendra OPC Private Limited on her own. She has been tutoring kids along with mentoring graduate and postgraduate students in academic and creative writing. On some days she is a dreamer while on others she is a realist. She firmly believes in humanism. Nature mesmerizes her.

She has initiated this project and has edited the book along with compiling it.

1. The Two Of Us

- Swarnika

I loved you enough
For the two of us,
And you couldn't give me
Even half of what I deserved.

.

I fought enough
For the two of us,
And instead, you started
Another war with me.

.

I held on enough
For the two of us,
And you decided to chop off
The strings that held us together.

.

I cared enough
For the two of us,
When you forgot to mention
I was so irreplaceable.

.

Perhaps I should have left you
For the two of us,
Saving one from the guilt
And the other from hurt.

2. I Guess It Was My Fault

– Swarnika

I guess it was my fault.

.

.

I guess it was my fault.
You kept hurting me,
And I let you.

.

.

I guess it was my fault.
You keep breaking me,
Piece by piece,
Shredding every ounce
Of my untethered skin,
And I let you.

.

.

I guess it was my fault.
You kept filling my world
With all your lies,
With all your fabrications,

With all your demands,
With all your expectations,
And I let you.

.

.

I guess it was my fault.
You ruined the idea of love for me,
And I let you.

3. Don't Romanticize The Idea Of Love

- Swarnika

Don't romanticize the idea of love,
There is nothing pleasant about it.
All it brings to the table
Is a world of hurt
Preached by disappointment.
Any heart that loved truly
Hasn't been spared by this.
Clutched in its claws
It picks you apart -
Atom by atom.
Perhaps this is what they meant
Would be the repercussion of
The fall of humans.
I bet Eve's fruit wasn't that good
To introduce earth
To this catastrophe.

4. Of Love

- *Swarnika*

The very idea of falling in love
Tells you that it is
Something ominous.

.

.

You don't rise.
You don't grow.
All you do is lose
The essence of life
And yourself.

.

.

You would probably get hurt.
Scraped and bruised,
It'll be hard to get up again.
And once you do,
It'll be hard
To trust another soul,
To fall for them again,
Because no one wants

To be lost
In this void
Of Love...

5. Stars and Scars

- Swarnika

I know that you're not here
Yet the heart pines
You still live in my heart rent-free
My thoughts entangled in grapevines.

.

Sometimes I lay down
Dreaming about going back in time
To hear your voice once again
I hope this ain't a crime.

.

Every time I move a step forward
I fall twice behind
Thinking about your love
That was shrewd and kind.

.

I know we weren't meant to be
But sometimes I wish upon falling stars
We would find our way back to each other
And not be reminded of these old scars.

6. She Makes My Heart Dance

- Swarnika

She makes my heart dance.

.

.

She makes my heart dance
In a way my feet never have,
Catching beats and
Skipping a few,
Living each moment
As something brand new.

.

She brought rhythm
To my life that was
utterly unsynchronized;
She brought grace,
She brought joy,
She became my world
Even before I realized.

7. I Write Love Songs

- *Swarnika*

I write love songs
In the ink of my blood
Oozing out the gaps
Of my broken heart.

.

These songs are not true.
They didn't happen.
They don't happen.
They are a figment
Of a fictional world,
Far from reality.

.

The sole purpose is
To entertain and please
The longing heart
That desires perfection
In this world,
Built on the foundation
Of imperfection.

.

These songs that I write,
Are written in words
That I don't believe
But kept hoping
To come true.
They didn't.

.

I perhaps scam people
Who listen to my songs
In the hope of knowing love,
Feeling what it really is.
I give them that
Their eyes want to read,
Their ears want to hear,
Their lips want to sing,
And their heart wants to believe.
I sell them the lie
That I was sold,
That I believed was true.

.

I tell them about this
Utopian idea of love,
And they don't realize that
They are getting tangled
In an idea that is maligned.
Utopia, afterall, is
A no man's world.

8. Hello and Goodbye

– Swarnika

Hello,
It has been some time
Since I reached out to you,
Since you reached out to me.

.

It has probably been longer
Since I got through you
And you got through me.

.

I just write here, not expecting any reply.
Our fate was destined, something we can't deny.
It is just that that I wanted to say it out
For the last time- clear and loud.

.

It sucks that things turned out the way they did
But that's okay now.
You are already doing better
And perhaps I soon will.

.

I wish you were more upfront then,

Things would have been clearer.
It would have been easier.
But that's okay 'cause
I understand

.

I understand where you're coming from.
I understand that it hasn't always been
Nice and comfortable, like home.
I understand that we weren't on the same page.
I understand that we were supposedly
Reading lines that dispersed with age.
I understand it was hard for you to realize.
I understand you couldn't express,
Feelings are hard to materialize.
I get it that you liked the company.
It just that I would have felt better
Knowing it was friendship, not destiny.
I know that it hasn't been easy for you.
But shouldn't you have empathized with me
As I kept getting hurt in the process too.

.

I kept waiting for a word from you
On those never-ending night.
Those ended but still there wasn't
Any word from you; perhaps
You were blinded to my plight.

.

You were hurt one day
And I stayed up all night
To be by your side.
I was broken on another
And you slept peacefully
While I cried all night.
You needed me
And I as there for you
Leaving everything behind.
I needed you once
And you said- "Talk to your friends,
Talking to me about this isn't kind."

.

Perhaps you just needed me
To feel better about yourself
But now that I know it all,
Clearer are the things I see.

.

I learnt a lot in the time we had.
I started loving myself more.
I'm thankful and not mad
Because I have become better than before.

.

There aren't any tears here
Not a distant sigh;
Love isn't in attendance where,
It is better to say goodbye.

9. Let Us Just Be Friends

- Swarnika

Let us just be friends.

Some things are better when they are left uncomplicated.

Let us be unchaotic.

Let us be easy to comprehend.

Let us just be friends.

Other titles have definitions that keep changing with time.

Let us be the constant,

In this world of variables.

Let us beat time.

Let us just be friends.

Let us find happiness,

And not our flaws.

Let us not idolize.

Let us not patronize.

Let us be happy.

Let us be inncent.

Let us be pure.

Let us not malign.

Let us just be friends.

10. Perhaps

- Swarnika

Don't play with my heart.
It is the one that beats for you;
Not the ones broken previously
By faces similar to yours.

.

It is weird
As every time it feels like
This is the one that would last
But it doesn't.
Every time it seems like
This is the last time I give away my heart
But it isn't.
Every time it looks like
I might not recover
But I do.
And every time I wish for
Never to love again
But I fall.

.

The idea of love makes me laugh.

How can something be so intense?
Perhaps it is all a pretence.
How can something be so confounding?
But then there exists the concept of rebounding.
Perhaps we are all just a bunch of messed up souls
Looking for someone to fill our heart's holes.
Perhaps we declare the feeling s that are unknown
In the fear of being left alone.
Or perhaps we don't need love at all
Just need to be happy and stand tall.

.

Perhaps you and I keep breaking these hearts
And they keep replenishing
Just like the cells in our body,
Making us eat our emotions
And feel our plates- half-empty.

Khushi Kaushik

Khushi Kaushik, the elder child in a nuclear family, was born and brought up in Faridabad, Haryana. She studied in DAV public school, sec 14, Faridabad, and was good in studies since childhood. She had a keen interest in studying literature. The author of 'Secret of room 333' is known for her flash fiction. She started writing her first book when she was 13, which is a very young age, her interest developed in the field of content writing and she started to write poems, stories and finally decided to write fiction. She is 20 at present and is pursuing English literature from the University of Delhi. Apart from being an author, she is a poetess as well and her compilation of romantic poems 'Shades of love' had a great readership. She is an eager learner and has various interests. She has a keen interest in art, she has been painting since childhood and is a very good singer as well and also has won competitions in singing. She has a dynamic personality and is someone who loves to take up new challenges and broaden her horizons.

11. My Love Died

- *Khushi Kaushik*

You are so distant
And yet to close
That I can feel your presence
Wherever I go,
With me it flows.
.

I can always sniff
The scent of your love
And sense your gentle touch
As if it came from above.
.

That soft embrace of yours
That gave me comfort
Is the only thing missing
In this despairing dead desert.
.

That moment is a memory
That I can't live again
It's not that I don't want to
But if I try to be brave

I shall feel relive the pain.

.

The pain of your separation
To see your breath fade
And ask lord why
The pain of all the questions.

.

So I shall pass on love
For I don't want the pain
That follows this bliss
In the end, it will all be in vain.

12. What Is It?

- Khushi Kaushik

What is love?
Is it pain or pleasure?
Or is it a package deal?
Is it ice creams and unicorns?
Or a mountain between the streets?
If it is selflessness as they say
Then why can I not see generosity?
True love is strongest they say
Then why do I see people leave?
Love has no boundaries they say
Then why are there walls?
It's divine is what I say
Then why isn't there peace in the halls?
I think the idea of love
Is too old, oddly written for us
As today in this world
It is no pure breed like the Erectus
Love has evolved with time
And have modernized so much
That we may say that

Love has long left us.
So what to we call this
Newly invented intimacy?
It definitely is not love
And neither is treachery.

13. The Flower Pot

- *Khushi Kaushik*

The red corals
Resemble your lips,
The soft petals
Feel like your kiss.

.

This perfect sepal
Represents your support,
And these green leaves
Remind me of your fort.

.

These shining pearls
Sitting on the leaves
Portray the beauty of
Your bright eyes.

.

This wet clay
Is brown as your hair,
These white marbles
Paint your smile here;
But hey! This ain't all.

All I told till now
Was only pretty things
And that I can't allow!

.

The big black stones
That lay here and there
But yet goes unseen
Because of the beauty everywhere;
They remind me of the flag,
The red flags I saw,
But charmed by your face
I was caught in your claw.

.

These thorns here
Are like spikes
But not on branches
And on a shaft.

.

Like the devil's stick
Similar to the morning star
Which you strike once
But it gives you infinite scar.

.

And it perfectly paints
Your betrayal towards me
I was blinded by the lights
And in the dark, you flee...

14. Our Song

- Khushi Kaushik

Oh! this song
Sounds like him -
This magical song!
.

We danced on it
Every time we met as if
The song was meant for us.
Oh! Here comes that beat
That beat when I rested my head
On his shoulder, feeling all the warmth.
.

Ahh! There comes that melody
Where we used to spin together
And sing out loud 'love is heavenly'.
.

Wait! I hear that tune
The tune where we stopped
And held each other like a spoon.
.

And oh! There comes the thump

Where we left our cozy space
And with all energy again jump.
.

Oh! This love song
Is not just words but feelings
As it is our song.

15. The Love

- *Khushi Kaushik*

For I have felt love before,
Had butterflies and unicorns,
But this is not the same.
This is not that love.

.

This is something that engulfs,
Absorbs out all my strength,
Make me the strongest vulnerable person,
And make me question who I am.

.

It doesn't pull or let me settle
But pushes me for more,
And when I fail it treasures me
But never let me forfeit.

.

This is not just love;
This admires and accelerate,
And elevate me to heaven.
This is eternal love.
This is the love!

16. Losing Self

- *Khushi Kaushik*

And when I see the stars,
I see a long-lost lost friend.
Quite familiar to me,
It never seemed to end.

.

But oh! The mirror doesn't lie,
I'm seeing a part descend.
And I am falling to trust
Because I can not bend.

.

I can't deliver my love
Because betrayal is what it lend,
And so all I do is wave;
Wave to the stars and my end.

.

Because yes I ain't the same;
I am beyond mend.

17. Unjust Destiny

- *Khushi Kaushik*

We have similar souls
But from different ages
And maybe that is why we find these differences.

.

My soul is too young
And creative yet stubborn;
Yours is too wise
And always in want to govern.

.

My soul is like water
That can not be held
While you like to own
Which makes me repelled.

.

You like to sit and read
While I want to fly
So you cut my wings
And all I could do is cry.

.

I wish I could leave;

You wish we didn't love.
Maybe we were destined
To see the sacrifice in love.

18. Strangers

- Khushi Kaushik

What was that love for?

All those butterflies?

All that sweet talk?

What was it for?

Why did you pretend?

Pretend to love me

When you were cleary out

In someone else's bed.

Why did you hurt me?

You could have just walked away

But you choose to stay

And break my soul slowly.

Well, I hear you are far,

Far from this land.

Yes we ain't talking

As we are strangers again.

19. My Love For You

- Khushi Kaushik

My love is honest,

So honest

That you can see my veins bleeding your name.

.

My love is deep,

So deep

That your breath brings me life.

.

My love is pure,

So pure

That I see heaven by looking in your eyes.

.

My love is true,

So true

That every pearl shed by your eye sheds my blood.

.

My love is trustworthy,

So trustworthy

That even heavens can swear on.

.

My love is intimate,

So intimate

That your curved lips make my adrenaline leak.

.

My love is selfless,

So selfless

That I'd die a thousand times for you.

.

But above all,

My love is miserable,

So miserable

That I love you even when you are not mine to love.

20. Heaven Into Hell

- *Khushi Kaushik*

You laid my eyes on me,

You said you love me,

You faked your care for me,

You gave your free time to me,

You suddenly decided to leave me...

You laughed at me

But

I still stand by you,

I still feel love when touched by you,

I still support you,

I still think at night about you,

I still wait for you...

You built a heaven for me

And turned it into hell...

Raman Singh

Raman Singh was born in the year 2001 in Haryana, India. He never did things to pass time, when he held on to a thing, he gave himself completely to it. May it be playing basketball for nine years, may it be doing theatre, which also induced interest in literature. He is currently pursuing a BA(Hons) in English, from Delhi University, and is an important part of the theatre society. He has also acted in six theatrical productions and has written several short plays and stories. Not to forget his love for Hindi Literature, which has added new dimensions to his imaginations and in which he finds those values and thoughts which otherwise would've been too late to discover. If there is anything else that he loves, that is a cup of coffee. His notion of feeling content and happy is to have a cup of coffee with a brownie while reading a book.

21. From Somewhere

- *Raman Singh*

Save Love somewhere
'Cause when the hour of grief would come
You would be sitting lonely in the woods somewhere.
It would be Love that would come
Flying far away from somewhere.
On a branch, they would sit,
Sing a song of Love from somewhere
And that should be it
To help you empty the grief from somewhere
And fill in Love from somewhere.

22. Love Will Rise

- Raman Singh

On Doomsday,

When everything will be burned

With the hateful fire of hate,

All around would be dark and silent,

Hopelessness would be echoing

In that ash ridden ground,

Smoke filled air-

It would wake up,

Slowly,

Without noise,

That would suck in all the hate in itself

A power called Love.

23. Right In Your Heart

- *Raman Singh*

Dear Love
I know you tried
But couldn't hide
Those warm tears you cried
Filled with a longing to see me by your side
When I bid you goodbye.
But to your surprise
I am not gone to some foreign land
I am holding your hand
Those castles aren't yet washed away by those concurring
waves
Which were made of sand.
Still wondering
Where I am?
Close your eyes, and
Take a deep breath
I will appear
Right in your heart.

24. Never Thought

- Raman Singh

Never thought
That glaze for me in your eyes
Would vanish this early
That warming affection from your heart
Would vanish this early
That exciting walk you walked with me from your legs
Would vanish this early
That smile upon seeing me from your lips
Would vanish this early
Never thought
I in You
Would vanish this early.
Cause you were the one
Who promised me to stay by my side
Hold my hand
Kiss my cheeks
Hug me tight
In my loneliest hour
You would be my aid.
Never thought

In that hour
I would need to find you.

25. People Of Love

- *Raman Singh*

Today

I saw a mother begging

No one gave any help.

Yesterday

I saw a six-year-old girl selling things

No one bought anything from.

Week before

I saw a teenage girl wiping windshields

Of cars stuck in a traffic jam

No one gave a penny.

Month before

I saw an adult girl showing tricks with a street magician

No one gave any attention.

Year before

I saw a woman lying on the road

Blood all over her body, and

People around her

To conclude,

People of Love were and are less.

26. Where Are You?

– Raman Singh

Where are you?
I who sowed your seeds everywhere I went
Demand to know
Where are you?
Don't find you on the streets
Where people fight, and
Throw abuses at each other
Don't find you in homes
Which are now turned to mere houses
Don't find you among my friends
Who are eaten up by jealousy
Don't find you on the internet
Where all is all showy-showy
Don't find you in people
Who are always running late
I don't get to see you in my life
So
Where are you?
I demand to know.

27. To Hug You

- *Raman Singh*

Of all the bodily pleasures

I choose to hug you

My body still remembers

Our first hug

How all the scenery disappeared

The moment I saw you

Arms open

We hugged so tightly

As if wanting to enter each other's body

Arms clenched

Not wanting to lose each other

Our hands patted a hundred times

Calming each other

Eyes rained all those tears

Which we didn't cry as we promised each other

Today, as I cry some of those tears

This last time

I only choose to hug you.

28. Cruel Distance

- *Raman Singh*

Oh, cruel Distance!
I have come to you with a request
Can you just disappear tomorrow?
"What for?" Said he arrogantly
It is her birthday
I wish to be with her tomorrow
And I cannot wait a single day more
Every night I scroll through her pictures
My heart screams to be with her
To hug her
To kiss her
To play with her hair
To sit in her lap
To caress her cheeks
To be with her
I am warning you
If I don't meet tomorrow and die
Then you would be the culpable
Just because of you
My heart aches

When I miss her
I sit and appear to be calm from outside
But it is only me who knows
The mad storm which rises inside
So full of strength
That I could overcome you and still wouldn't be tired
But I am calmly requesting you
When I wake up tomorrow
Just disappear.

29. Love is Acceptance

- Raman Singh

A dark room
In which no light enters
Everything has a layer of dust
Whose particles are full of
Sadness
Loneliness
They all wear a worn-out expression
Smell rot
I am sitting in that room
But to me comes the scented smell of roses
Warm, comforting sunrays relax my facial muscles
Sweet like sugar a voice is caught by my ears
Ups and downs make a tune so tempting
As if specially curated for me
I walk towards it
Unlike other voices
This one comes from a sensitive heart
Hearing which
My heart thinks of beating again
Upon reaching

A tall, wide blossoming with flowers of the color of acceptance
Tree stands there
That melodious voice leaves the room of my ears
Assured of completing its work
I stand still
and cry a million tears
The land below soaks up all those tears
No one asks me to stop crying
Finally
I feel accepted.

30. In The End

- Raman Singh

There is a pattern
There are thousands of it
In different eras different people created it
Thousands live according to the pattern
Some protect you in life
Some help you earn in life
Some make you live an honest life
But they all are so less of Life
Because their pattern doesn't end with
What we need in the end
A pattern that is full of life
Start with love
Ends with love
Because
In the end, all we need is Love.

www.ingramcontent.com/pod-product-compliance
Lightning Source LLC
Chambersburg PA
CBHW020933160726
47993CB00007B/2766